D0290936

A Little Book about

Confession for Children

———————————— • ————————————

Kendra Tierney

A Little Book about
Confession for Children

Illustrations: Maria Ashton

MAGNIFICAT · Ignatius

This book is dedicated
to Fr. Juan Velez, who asked me to write it,
to my son, who asked the tough questions,
to my husband, who made sure I finished it,
and to my father, who always knew I had it in me. Kendra

To my parents, Charles and Marita Goering,
with love and gratitude. Maria

Kendra Tierney writes a Catholic blog at:
www.CatholicAllYear.com

Nihil Obstat: Fr. Michael J. Barrett, S.T.D.
                Censor

Imprimatur: ✠ Most Reverend José H. Gomez
                Archbishop of Los Angeles
                April 1, 2015

Contents

A Note to Parents 7

Some Words to Know 12

Questions and Answers for Children and Their Parents 15
   1. Children don't commit really bad sins, so why would I need
       to go to confession? 15
   2. What if I'm scared to go to confession? 16
   3. Can't I just pray to God directly? Why do I need a priest? 16
   4. What if the priest tells someone else my sins? 19
   5. What is sin, anyway? 19
   6. What does original sin have to do with me? 21
   7. Another kind of sin? 21
   8. How can I know whether a particular sin is mortal or venial? 22
   9. Sometimes it's hard for me to forgive people,
       so how can I be sure God will forgive me? 25
  10. I want to ask God for his forgiveness, but how do I do it? 27
  11. What does going to confession do? 28
  12. How does the Sacrament of Reconciliation help me to avoid
       sin in the future? 30
  13. How do I receive the Sacrament of Penance? 31
  14. How do I remember my sins? 31
  15. How can I be sorry for my sins? 33
  16. How can I make up my mind not to commit those sins again? 34
  17. How do I tell my sins to the priest? 36

18. What is the penance the priest gives me? 37

19. What do I do after confession? 37

20. How often should I go to confession? 37

21. Please explain the examination of conscience. 38

22. How can I know what God's rules are? 39

23. What if I'm still worried about going to confession? 41

24. What is a saint? 42

Saint John Vianney, 43. Saint John Bosco, 44. Saint Pio, 45. Saint Mary Magdalene, 46. Saint Josemaria Escriva, 48.

An Examination of Conscience 51

The Sacrament of Penance, a Review 62

A Note to Parents

The Sacrament of Penance is often misunderstood, by children and adults alike. If your child is preparing for his first confession, it's easy for you both to feel overwhelmed. Or if first confession was a while ago, perhaps you wish your child had a better understanding of the sacrament.

The following questions and answers are the result of my own experiences as I helped my son to prepare for his first confession. In my quest to answer all of his questions, I ended up filling in a lot of gaps in my own knowledge of Church teaching, and now we both have a much better understanding of this beautiful sacrament.

I encourage you to learn along with your child and to use this opportunity to teach the real wisdom of our Church, not a watered-down version. If your child doesn't learn it now, when will he learn it? If you don't teach it to him, who will?

Pope Paul VI wrote, "Since parents have given children their life, they are bound by the most serious obligation to educate their offspring and therefore must be recognized as the primary and principal educators."[1]

As parents it is our responsibility to educate our children. Of course, schools and parishes often provide excellent instruction, but let us not forget that God has given these children to us, and we are accountable for how much they know or don't know about their faith.

And if we're going to teach them anything, let's have it be the real thing. Our children are capable of learning and understanding a much deeper faith in God than is often entrusted to them. We want them to have a real and lasting friendship with Jesus that will help them throughout their lives. We also want them to have the answers they will need when they are confronted by doubts or by those who do not share their faith.

I hope that what we have learned can help your family too.

How to Use This Book

Set aside a few minutes each day to discuss a few of these questions with your child. You may want to read the whole book before you get started. In any case, make sure to leave time for discussion.

....

1. Pope Paul VI, *Gravissium educationis*, Declaration on Christian education, Vatican Web site, October 28, 1965, http://www.vatican.va/archive/hist_councils/ii_vatican_council/documents/vat-ii_decl_19651028_gravissimum-educationis_en.html

If your child asks you a question that you don't know the answer to, congratulations! You've got a child who's paying attention. Be honest with your child and say, "That is a great question. I don't know the answer to it, but I will find out and let you know."

Then, do it! Read ahead in this book if you haven't done so already, ask a trusted friend or priest, or seek a faithful Catholic book or website. Figure it out for yourself; then explain it to your child.

Occasionally, a child will ask a question that seems to require an answer that he isn't ready to understand. I like first to turn the difficult question around and ask the child what he thinks about it. I have often found that what he was really asking was much less complicated than I had thought!

But if the difficult question would require a difficult answer, I instead give a short and simple answer and then say, "We can talk more about this when you're a little bit older."

The footnotes at the bottom of some of these pages refer to the *Catechism of the Catholic Church*. It is a wonderful resource, and every Catholic home should have one.

Other footnotes refer to the Bible, and every Catholic home should have one of these as well. Not any Bible will do; make sure it's a Catholic edition (other Bibles leave out several books). Ignatius Press publishes several very good ones; I also like the Navarre Bible, and the New American Bible, published by the United States Conference of Catholic Bishops.

Once you've read through and discussed this whole book with your child, keep it someplace where he'll be able to reach it.

Make a habit of going to confession yourself and take your child with you. Catholics should go to confession when they have committed a serious sin. But we can benefit from confessing our lesser sins too, and the Church strongly recommends that we do so.

Many faithful Catholics go to confession once a month, or even once a week. It is especially important to make a good confession before Easter and Christmas.

Before going to confession, a person should make an examination of conscience. One designed for children is provided in this book beginning on page 51. Your child can start asking himself the questions provided on the back flip of this book, and write out if he wants to what he needs to confess on a piece of paper. After confession, he can burn it in the fireplace or shred it in a shredder. The idea is to make the point that the sins are really gone now that they have been forgiven by God.

It is very important to respect the privacy of your child's confession. If your child wishes to discuss his sins with you that's wonderful, but never ask him to tell you his sins or to show you those he has written down. You might, however, need to remind your child to do the penance he was given by the priest. After confession, it's a nice tradition to go out for a small treat, such as ice cream. This helps children to have positive associations with the experience and reinforces the sweetness of God's mercy!

Some Words to Know

————— • —————

ABSOLUTION: The prayer by which the priest, in the name of Jesus, takes away from us the guilt and punishment we would otherwise deserve for our sins.

CONFESSION: Voluntarily telling our sins to a priest in order to have them forgiven by God.

CONTRITION: Sorrow for having offended God by our sins. Sometimes this includes the feeling of sorrow, but sometimes it doesn't, which is fine as long as we have made the decision to be sorry for doing what we know is wrong.

EXAMINATION OF CONSCIENCE: When we calmly think over the days since our last confession and recall any times we have done things that offend God and hurt ourselves and others.

GRACE: The free gift that God gives us of filling our souls with love for Him and for others. We get grace from participating in the sacraments, and grace is what helps us to be good and to love God more and more.

PENANCE: The prayers or actions assigned to us by the priest after we have confessed our sins. These help us undo the harm done by our sins.

PENITENT: The person who confesses his sins.

RECONCILIATION: Becoming friends again with God after we have damaged that friendship through serious sin.

SACRAMENT: A sign or ceremony, instituted by Christ, that we can experience with our senses (we can see or hear or touch or taste it) and by which God puts grace into our souls.

SACRAMENT OF CONFESSION, SACRAMENT OF PENANCE, AND SACRAMENT OF RECONCILIATION: These are all different terms for the same thing—the sacrament that forgives sins committed after Baptism. Like the other sacraments, this is an outward sign instituted by Christ to give us his grace. It includes confession, penance, and reconciliation. The different names just emphasize different parts of the sacrament.[2]

....

2. Fr. John Hardon, *Modern Catholic Dictionary* (Intermirifica, 1999)

Questions and Answers for Children and Their Parents

———— • ————

1. Children don't commit really bad sins, so why would I need to go to confession?

Jesus said, "Let the children come to me, and do not hinder them; for to such belongs the kingdom of heaven."[3] Jesus gave us confession not as a punishment but as a gift. He wants us all to accept this gift so that we can be close to him and receive the healing and peace that come from his mercy. Making regular use of this sacrament helps us to become holy and to go to heaven.

....

3. Matthew 19:14

2. What if I'm scared to go to confession?

Confession isn't meant to be scary. It is a meeting with Jesus, who loves you and wants to be your friend. Pope John Paul II called the reconciliation that we receive from confession "a merciful gift of God to humanity."[4] This book can help us figure out why.

3. Can't I just pray to God directly? Why do I need a priest?

Of course you can ask God to forgive your sins, and you should. Since Jesus is God, he had the power to forgive sins. He gave that power to his Apostles when after his Resurrection he breathed on them and said, "Receive the Holy Spirit. If you forgive the sins of any, they are forgiven; if you retain the sins of any, they are retained."[5] Priests today still have this power given to them by Jesus. Jesus wanted us to confess our sins to God, through the church.

Forgivess of sins was very important to Jesus. In fact, he told us that a healthy soul is even more important than a healthy body. In the Bible we find a story about this.[6]

Jesus was visiting someone's home, and as you can imagine lots of people went there to see him. A paralyzed man ("para-

....

4. Pope John Paul II, *Reconciliation and Penance*, Vatican Web Site, December 2, 1984, http://www.vatican.va/holy_father/john_paul_ii/apost_exhortations/documents/hf_jp-ii_exh_02121984_reconciliatio-et-paenitentia_en.html
5. John 20:22-23
6. Mark 2:1-12

lyzed" means that his legs didn't work) was brought to the house by his friends so that Jesus could heal him, but the house was so crowded that they couldn't get near Jesus.

These friends didn't give up. They climbed to the top of the house with the paralyzed man on his stretcher and opened up a hole in the roof above where Jesus was. Then they lowered the man down.

Jesus saw that this man and his friends must have had great faith, for they went to so much trouble to see him. Of course, everyone expected Jesus to heal the man. But what he said was, "My son, your sins are forgiven."

Some people were angry with Jesus for saying this, because they didn't believe that he was really God, who alone can forgive sins.

To show them that he does have the power to forgive sins, Jesus then healed the paralyzed man's body. The man stood up, picked up his mat, and walked home.

Like the paralyzed man, we need Jesus to heal us. We especially need him to heal our souls through the forgiveness of our sins. In order to let him do this for us, we can go to confession, because Jesus has empowered the priest to forgive sins on his behalf. We can imitate the paralyzed man's friends by bringing our friends to confession too!

Since Reconciliation is a sacrament, it gives us grace, that is, the gift of God's own strength. It gives us not only forgiveness but also the strength to help us to avoid sin in the future.

Plus, Reconciliation helps us to believe that our sins are truly forgiven because we hear the priest forgive us out loud.

When we are willing to admit our sins and to ask for forgiveness through the Church, it helps us out in the "real world"[7] too. When we are able to become friends again with God, it helps us to become friends again with the people we may have hurt through our sins, even small sins.

....

7. *Catechism of the Catholic Church (CCC)*, 1455

4. What if the priest tells someone else my sins?

The priest will never, never, never tell anyone else anything that you have told him in confession—**no matter what**.[8]

And remember, the priest knows what you are going through. He doesn't just listen to other people's confessions, he goes to confession himself too! Every priest you know goes to confession with another priest. Even the Pope goes to confession! He's happy you're there and wants to help you.

5. What is sin, anyway?

Sin is disobedience to God. Adam and Eve committed the first sin on earth when they disobeyed God in the Garden of Eden.[9]

When God created Adam and Eve, he wanted them to be happy. He told them they could eat the fruit from any tree in the garden except one.

In the form of a serpent, Satan came to Eve and told her that the fruit from that tree was good, and that eating it would make her like God.

Eve believed Satan's lies. She ate the fruit and gave some to Adam. They did not love God enough to follow his rules. They loved pleasing themselves more than they loved God. This was the first sin ever committed on earth, which is the reason it is called the original sin.

....

8. *CCC*, 2490
9. Genesis 3:1-13

6. What does original sin have to do with me?

Adam and Eve are our first parents. And just as your parents may have passed on something to you, like brown eyes or a good singing voice, the state that Adam and Eve fell into when they committed the first sin has been passed on to each of us. We are born with original sin, which means we are born in a weakened condition.[10]

That's the bad news.

But the good news is that the Sacrament of Baptism washes away original sin and gives us a fresh, clean soul filled with the grace of God.[11]

We didn't commit original sin; Adam and Eve did. But that's not the only type of sin. There is also another kind of sin.

7. Another kind of sin?

Yes. It's called actual sin, which is a sin we commit ourselves. Unfortunately, while baptism takes away our original sin, it does NOT take away our inclination or ability to do bad things on our own.[12] There are two types of actual sin: mortal sin and venial sin.

Mortal sin is a BIG sin committed on purpose. It is BIG because it turns our soul from God completely. That's why it is

....

10. *CCC*, 404
11. *CCC*, 1263
12. *CCC*, 1426

called a deadly sin. People who have committed a mortal sin are not allowed to receive Holy Communion. But even more importantly, if they die without being sorry for this sin they can't go to heaven.[13] Children don't usually commit mortal sins, but grown-ups sometimes do.

Kids usually commit the other kind of actual sin: venial sin. Venial sin is a little sin. It's not as bad as mortal sin.[14] It doesn't kill our souls, but it does make our souls sick to do on purpose what is not good.

8. How can I know whether a particular sin is mortal or venial?

There is no one list of sins to tell us which ones are mortal and which ones are venial. There are some sins that the Church tells us are always serious sins, but we also have to consider the circumstances in which they were committed.

To figure out whether a sin is a mortal sin or a venial sin, we should ask ourselves these three questions:

1. Is the sin serious?
2. Does the sinner know that it is serious?
3. Does the sinner fully consent to the sin?

....
13. *CCC*, 1035
14. *CCC*, 1862

To understand the first question we need to know how to tell if something is a "grave matter." All sins forbidden by the Ten Commandments are grave.

The commandments tell us in general what is a grave matter, but how serious a sin is can vary depending on such things as whether people have been seriously harmed by the sin and what was the intention behind it.

The second question reminds us that we cannot accidently commit a mortal sin. We must understand that we are committing a serious sin and decide to do it anyway.

The third question tells us that only a freely chosen act can be a mortal sin. A sin is not mortal if we commit it because we are scared or we are forced to do it. It also might not be mortal if we commit it because we have a bad habit and lack the will power to resist it.

In the last case, we need to understand that it is our responsibility to try to strengthen our will to resist temptation and to avoid situations and people that tempt us to sin.

If we can answer yes to all three of the above questions, then the sin is a mortal sin. If we answer no to at least one of these questions, then the sin is a venial sin, or in some cases it may not be a sin at all.

We will learn more about God's commandments later in the book, but let's look at a few examples of how circumstances can affect the seriousness of sins against them.

To dishonor your mother or your father is a sin against the fourth commandment. So, if your mom tells you to do your homework and you don't do it, you are committing a sin. If you are simply being lazy and do not want to harm your mother, you are likely committing a venial sin. But say a rebellious teenager refuses to stay home to finish his homework with an outburst intended to hurt his mother. Such behavior could be mortal sin.

Hurting someone physically is a sin against the fifth commandment. To hit someone unthinkingly (unless it's for self-defense) is a venial sin. But to punch him in the face in order to hurt him (unless it's for self-defense) could be a mortal sin.

Stealing is a sin against the seventh commandment. While theft is always a grave matter, stealing a piece of candy is not as serious as robbing a bank, or stealing food when you are poor and hungry is not the same as when you are rich!

Lying about other people is a sin against the eighth commandment. If Kevin is mad because Billy beat him in a race and dishonestly tells his friends that Billy cheated, he would be committing a venial sin.

But what if Kevin's friends tell the coach what they have heard and he cuts Billy from the track team? What if Kevin still doesn't tell the truth, even though he knows that something serious has happened to Billy as a result of his lie? Kevin is now committing a more serious sin.

The best way to be sure if a particular sin is a serious one, is to ask a priest about it.

9. *Sometimes it's hard for me to forgive people, so how can I be sure God will forgive me?*

God's love for you is infinite. That means it is so big that it has no end; it's bigger than we could ever imagine. There is nothing you could do that God couldn't forgive.[15]

In the Bible, Jesus told a story to his friends to help them understand God's mercy. The story is about a man and his two sons.[16]

The younger son asks his father to give him his inheritance (the money he would get after his father dies), and he goes off to another country. There he spends all his money on parties and bad behavior.

Once his money is all gone, he takes a job feeding pigs. He realizes that he has been very foolish and decides to go home, where he will apologize to his father and ask if he may work for him as a hired servant.

While he is still a long way off, his father sees him walking toward home and runs out to hug him.

The son says, "Father, I have sinned against heaven and before you; I am no longer worthy to be called your son."

But before he can even finish talking, his father gives him new clothes and shoes and has a wonderful dinner made for him.

....

15. *CCC*, 982
16. Luke 15:11-32

He says, "Let us eat and make merry; for this my son was dead, and is alive again; he was lost, and is found."

This is how God acts when we are truly sorry for our sins and ask for his forgiveness. He welcomes us back with open arms. Knowing that we hurt God when we sin, we go to him expecting anger and punishment. But what he gives us instead are new clothes and a party!

God doesn't ask us to become perfect before we come to him. The father in Jesus' story comes out to welcome his son "while he was yet at a distance."

God wants to forgive us and to celebrate with us even if we have faults that we need to work on. God's forgiveness is bigger than our biggest sin. His love is stronger than our weaknesses.

All he asks is that we come to him in the Sacrament of Reconciliation, really sorry for our sins and ready to do better.

10. *I want to ask God for his forgiveness, but how do I do it?*

By receiving the Sacrament of Penance or Reconciliation. Often this is called going to confession.[17]

....
17. *CCC*, 1424

11. What does going to confession do?

The Sacrament of Penance heals our souls when we hurt them by sinning. When we confess our sins to a priest, it is God who hears us and forgives our sins.[18] God always forgives us if we are sorry, no matter how big or how many our sins are.

The Bible tells us the story of how Jesus treated a woman who had committed a big sin.[19] She had been arrested, and the people were going to throw rocks at her.

Jesus came and told the people, "Let him who is without sin among you be the first to throw a stone at her." One by one the people put down their rocks and left.

When only Jesus and the woman were left he told her, "Go, and do not sin again."

God always forgives us when we ask, but he also asks us to change our behavior. The Sacrament of Penance helps us with this.[20]

....
18. *CCC*, 1461
19. John 8:3-11
20. *CCC*, 1468

12. How does the Sacrament of Reconciliation help me to avoid sin in the future?

The Sacrament of Reconciliation not only gives us the forgiveness of our sins, but also fills our souls with God's grace. This helps us grow in the virtues of faith, hope, and love.

• **Faith** is belief in God and in the teachings of the Catholic Church.

• **Hope** is the desire to receive the mercy and everlasting life that God has promised us and the trust that he will provide them.

• **Love** (or **charity**) is the love we give God with our whole heart and soul and the love that God asks us to give our neighbor.

We call these three virtues "theological virtues",[21] which is a fancy way of saying that they come from God. We cannot get them by our own efforts alone. We can seek them and try to practice them, but we receive them as a free gift from God.

The main way that God gives us grace is through the reception of the sacraments. Some sacraments, such as Baptism and Holy Orders, can only be received once.

Others, like Penance and Holy Eucharist (also called Communion) can and should be received often to allow us to continue to grow in the virtues.

Finally, we can go to any priest for confession, even to one who doesn't speak the same language we do! But the best practice

....

21. *CCC*, 1813

is to see the same priest regularly. He will get to know us, and get to know our strengths and weaknesses. He will be best able to give us advice and encouragement.

13. *How do I receive the Sacrament of Penance?*

We receive the Sacrament of Penance by doing the following:

1. **Remember our sins.**
2. **Be sorry for our sins.**
3. **Tell our sins to a priest.**
4. **Receive the Absolution of the priest.**
5. **Do the penance he gives us.**[22]

14. *How do I remember my sins?*

We remember sins by making an examination of conscience.[23] This is when we calmly think over the days since our last confession and recall any times we have done things that offend God and hurt ourselves and others.

We offend God and hurt ourselves and others when we break the Ten Commandments.

As you do your examination of conscience, you can write down the sins you would like to confess. We must remember to confess *our own* sins, not what we think are our parents'

....

22. *CCC*, 1491
23. *CCC*, 1493

or our friends' or our siblings' sins. It's best not to mention other people by name if we don't have to. We should also focus on actions, not tendencies. So we don't say, "I was lazy." Instead we say, "I didn't set the table when Mom asked me to."

15. *How can I be sorry for my sins?*

The best way to be truly sorry for our sins is to think about Jesus' sufferings. We call these sufferings his Passion. Jesus suffered and died on the Cross because of our sins. He did not sin, but we do. Jesus loves us so much that he wanted to suffer for our sins.[24] If we really think about Jesus' Passion, we will be sorry for the ways we have disobeyed God.

The sincere sorrow for having offended God (who loves us so much) is called contrition.

Contrition should come with a firm intention of not committing those sins again. We might not cry or even feel very sad about our sins, but if we wish that we hadn't done whatever it was, we are sorry.

There are two types of contrition: perfect and imperfect.

Perfect contrition is being sorry for our sins because we know that they have offended God. This is the best kind of contrition.

Imperfect contrition is being sorry for our sins only because we have hurt other people by doing them, or because we are afraid

....
24. *CCC*, 1451

of God's punishments.

If we have at least imperfect contrition, we can go to confession worthily.

16. How can I make up my mind not to commit those sins again?

Making up our minds not to commit those sins again means that we promise not to commit them again. This might seem impossible, but it is what we hope for.

Of course, God knows that we are weak, and he is happy if we try hard not to commit the same sins again. We get better at avoiding sin by developing good habits.

For example, perhaps we cheated on our homework when we were tired and wanted to go to bed. To keep from committing this sin again, we can make a point of beginning our homework before dinner, so that we will have plenty of time to finish and we won't be tempted to cheat.

Or perhaps we have sinned by breaking family rules while hanging out with a particular friend.

We should try to avoid people and places that make us want to sin, also called the "near occasion of sin".

Receiving the Sacrament of Penance gives us strength to resist temptation.[25]

....
25. *CCC*, 1496

If we do struggle often with one particular sin, it's a good idea to mention that to the Priest during confession. We should tell him whether we think we have done better or worse than usual in resisting the temptation to commit that sin. Then, the Priest will be better able to give us good advice on how to do better in the future.

17. How do I tell my sins to the priest?

We may kneel in a confessional and talk to the priest through a screen, or we may sit down face to face with the priest. Either way, the priest is happy to help you if you can't remember what to do; just ask him.[26] Also, you can bring this book with you.

Then you follow these simple steps:

1. The priest will greet you.

2. Make the Sign of the Cross and say, **Bless me Father, for I have sinned**.

3. The priest will invite you to trust in God. Then you say, **It has been (the number of weeks or months) since my last confession**.

4. The priest may read or say by heart some words from Scripture.

5. **You tell your sins to the priest.** You may look at your list.

6. The priest will give you some advice on how to be better, then give you your penance.

7. When the priest asks you to, **say the Act of Contrition** (it's best to have it memorized, but you can read it if necessary).

8. The priest will then give you the absolution. You receive absolution by crossing yourself and saying **Amen**.

9. After the absolution, the priest continues: "Give thanks to the Lord, for he is good."

You answer: **His mercy endures for ever**.

....

26. *CCC*, 1465

10. After the priest dismisses you, leave the confessional and do your penance immediately.

18. *What is the penance the priest gives me?*

The penance the priest gives us is an action that can help us to undo the harm our sins have done to ourselves and others. Often the priest asks us to say some prayers, but sometimes he asks us to do something else, for example, he might ask us to apologize to someone.[27] It is important to do the penance the priest gives us as soon as possible.

19. *What do I do after confession?*

After confession we should go to a pew in the church to say any prayers the priest has given us for penance. While at prayer, we should thank Jesus for suffering and dying for our sins. We should thank God for his mercy and ask him to help us to be better. If we remember a sin that we forgot to confess, we should know that it too has been forgiven.

20. *How often should I go to confession?*

We must not receive Holy Communion if we are in a state of mortal sin. So if we have committed a serious sin, we must receive

....
27. *CCC*, 1460

the Sacrament of Reconciliation as soon as possible, and certainly before we go to Communion. But that's not usually a problem for children.

How often should a person who hasn't committed a mortal sin go to confession? As Catholics we must confess our sins at least once a year,[28] but the Church recommends that we go more frequently than that. Some saints have suggested that we go once a month.

Most parishes offer the Sacrament of Reconciliation on a regular schedule, often Saturday afternoons, but you can always ask a priest to meet with you for confession at another time.

You can find out when your parish offers confession by calling, looking in the church bulletin, or checking the parish website.

21. Please explain the examination of conscience.

An examination is when you take a close look at something. Your conscience tells you what is right and wrong; it is God's voice that speaks to you inside about what you should do and what you should not do.

To make an examination of conscience, look over your past behavior to see if any things you have done or have failed to do offend God by breaking the rules he has given us for our good.[29] You will find an examination of conscience made just for kids beginning on page 51 of this book.

....

28. *CCC*, 2042
29. *CCC*, 1454

22. How can I know what God's rules are?

That one's easy. God's rules are his Commandments: the Ten Commandments God gave Moses in the Old Testament and the New Commandment Jesus gave us in the New Testament when he said, "As I have loved you, so you also should love one another." To find out if we have sinned, we can look at these commandments and ask ourselves questions about them.

GOD'S COMMANDMENTS

The New Commandment: Love one another. As I have loved you, so you also should love one another.

If you really love God, it will show in the way you treat the people around you.

The Ten Commandments

1. I am the LORD your God, you shall have no other gods before me.

Put God first in your life.

2. You shall not take the Name of the LORD your God in vain.

Be faithful to God in your words and in your promises.

3. Keep holy the Sabbath day.

Rest from work and go to Mass every Sunday and holy day of obligation.

4. Honor your father and your mother.

Follow the rules your parents give you; always treat them with respect.

5. You shall not kill.

Avoid behavior that could physically harm anyone, including yourself.

6. You shall not commit adultery.

Show proper respect for the human body and for marriage. Be modest.

7. You shall not steal.

Respect the property of others; get things only in an honest way.

8. You shall not bear false witness.

Always tell the truth about other people.

9. You shall not covet your neighbor's wife.

Be respectful of other people's relationships and grateful for your own.

10. You shall not covet your neighbor's goods.

Be content with what you have, and be grateful for the things that God and other people have given you.

23. What if I'm still worried about going to confession?

If we are ever feeling worried or unsure about confession, prayer is a great place to start feeling better. Jesus promises to forgive us and to give us peace. Ask him for that peace.

If we don't understand the Sacrament of Penance (even after reading this book) or we understand that it's important but we still don't feel like actually doing it, the first step is to ask God to give us the gift of understanding confession and the desire to go to confession.

God does not want us to be unhappy. Often the best way to start doing what God wants us to do is simply to ask him to help us want what he wants.

We have plenty of great examples of people from all over the world and all different walks of life, who were able to give their hearts and their lives completely to God. We call them saints.

24. What is a saint?

A saint is a person in heaven. Every person who has died and gone to heaven is a saint.

Most saints probably lived very quiet lives here on earth, and so we don't know their names. But some people lived such good lives that the Church can say with certainty that they are in heaven with God.

The saints give us the examples of their lives to help us know how to love God and our neighbor.

They also help us by their intercession, which means their prayers for us. If we ask them to, the saints before God will ask him to help us.[30]

Perhaps you have asked a friend to pray for you, or someone has asked you to pray for him. We know that God listens to our prayers for other people as well as those for ourselves. We also know that God listens especially to his special friends the saints.

There are many, many saints that the Church has made known to us, and we should try to get to know as many of them as we can, but a few have a special connection to confession. Let's learn about them.

....
30. *CCC*, 956

SAINT JOHN VIANNEY

Do you sometimes have trouble in school? Well, you already have something in common with our first saint.

Saint John Vianney was not a very good student. He even failed a test he took to get into the seminary (a school that trains young men to become priests). He tried again, and was able to pass. He completed his studies and was ordained a priest.

Saint John Vianney, pray for us!

He became the parish priest in a small village in France. He worked to teach children the Catholic faith and to bring their parents back to the practice of religion. He devoted time to charity work, for example he started an orphanage for girls.

He spent a big part of each day hearing confessions. He began by hearing the confessions of the people in his village, but then people started coming to him from other parishes, and eventually from all over the country, to confess their sins and to listen to his advice. In the last years of his life he would spend sixteen to eighteen hours a day in the confessional. In one year he heard over twenty thousand confessions!

People loved to come to see him because of his common sense and good judgment, but God also sometimes gave him the special gift of knowing about sins that people had been too worried to say out loud in their confession.

Despite his popularity and the great respect people had for him, he was always a very humble man.

Saint John Bosco, pray for us!

SAINT JOHN BOSCO

Have you ever had a really kind and wonderful teacher or coach? Then maybe you know what it would have been like to know our next saint.

Saint John Bosco had a very great love for children, especially the troublemakers! He spent his life teaching and caring for children that no one else loved. He helped them to accept God's love and to leave sin behind.

When John Bosco was just nine years old he had a dream. He was in a field among a group of wild young boys. They started misbehaving, and John jumped into the crowd and started fighting them and shouting to make them stop.

Then young John saw a vision of Jesus. In John's dream, Jesus told him that he must lead these boys, not by fighting but by kindness and gentleness.

John Bosco never forgot this dream and when he became a priest he dedicated his life to the care of orphans (children who have lost both parents through death). He set up schools to teach them about God and to train them for jobs. His mother helped him by cooking for the boys and sewing and washing their clothing.

He gained the trust of these wild boys as Jesus had told him to, with kindness and gentleness, rather than through the harsh punishments common in schools of his time.

He encouraged the children to attend Mass daily and to receive the Sacrament of Penance often. We can ask Saint John Bosco to help us grow in understanding as we prepare to receive the Sacrament of Penance.

SAINT PIO

Have you ever been really embarrassed about something? Then you can sympathize with our next saint, and he can sympathize with you.

Saint Pio knew he was going to be a priest from a very early age. He was only five years old when he privately devoted his life to Jesus, and only fifteen years old when he left home to become a priest.

Beginning at age twenty-three and continuing for most of the rest of his life, Padre Pio was given by God a very

Saint Pio, pray for us!

special kind of suffering called the stigmata. In his hands and feet he bore wounds like those Jesus suffered during his crucifixion.

Padre Pio didn't mind the pain from the wounds, but he was very embarrassed by all the attention he received because of them. He prayed that God would take away the visible wounds so that he could suffer in secret, but that was not God's plan for him.

Like Saint John Vianney, Padre Pio was a very gifted and popular confessor. Especially because he was so well known, sinners and holy people alike flocked to his confessional.

He encouraged people who came to see him to become more holy by weekly confession and daily Communion. He also advised daily spiritual reading, meditation (which is quietly thinking about God), and examination of conscience

He encouraged people to live by his motto: "Pray, hope, and don't worry." It would be a good motto for us all.

Saint
Mary Magdalene,
pray for us!

SAINT MARY MAGDALENE

Have you ever worried that you're not good enough to be friends with Jesus? Well, just wait until you hear about this saint.

Saint Mary Magdalene is known as the "Penitent". A penitent is a person who is sorry for something, but it is also the word we use to describe the person who goes to confession.

She lived at the time of Jesus and had lived a sinful life before she first met the Lord. She was beautiful and proud, but when she saw Jesus, she felt very sorry for all of her sins and knew she had to change her life.[31]

She came to see him while he was having dinner at the home of a rich man, and she knelt at his feet and cried over her sins. She washed Jesus' feet with her tears and dried them with her hair.

Many people were shocked that Jesus would let such a sinful woman even touch Him. But Jesus knew that Mary was truly sorry for her sins. He said to the people, "Her sins, which are many, are forgiven, for she loved much; but he who is forgiven little, loves little."

Then he said to her, "Your faith has saved you, go in peace."From that day on, Mary Magdalene was part of the group of holy women who served Jesus and the Apostles.

She was there with Jesus' Mother, Mary, and Saint John at the foot of the Cross when Jesus was crucified.[32]

Early on Easter morning, Mary Magdalene went to the tomb where they had laid Jesus' body after he had died on the Cross. She was the one who found the stone rolled away from the tomb.[33]

As she sat outside of the tomb weeping, Jesus himself appeared to her.

Jesus favored Mary Magdalene, the repentant sinner, with the gift of being the first of all of Jesus' friends to see him raised from the dead.[34]

....

31. Luke 7-8
32. Luke 23:49
33. John 20:1
34. John 20:11-18

Saint
Josemaria Escriva,
pray for us!

SAINT JOSEMARIA ESCRIVA

Are you worried that going to confession will be hard or scary? Our last saint is sure to make you feel better.

Saint Josemaria Escriva was born in Spain. He lived recently enough that there are photographs and even videos of him. So don't think that becoming a saint is only for people who lived hundreds of years ago!

When Saint Josemaria was a little boy, he was excited to have his first confession, but he was worried that the penance he would receive from the priest would be too hard to do. He thought perhaps he would have to say many, many prayers or do extra chores.

But when he got home from the church he told his mother and father that the priest had told him that for his penance he should get to eat a fried egg!

That might not be your idea of a reward, but in little Josemaria's house it was considered a special treat. And it certainly isn't hard to do! But even eating a fried egg, if we do it for God, can be a way of showing him that we wish to be better.

Josemaria always remembered his surprise penance, and it helped him never to forget how much Jesus loves us and wants to heal us in the Sacrament of Penance.

When Saint Josemaria grew up, he became a priest. He often talked to people about how important it is to go to confession regularly.

He also had some very good advice about how to confess your sins.

If Saint Josemaria were talking to you now, he might say, "Imagine you were carrying a big heavy rock in your arms, and some pebbles in your pockets. Now imagine that you had to walk for a long, long way. When you finally got where you were going, which would you put down first?"

You would certainly answer: "The rock first! Then the pebbles!"

Saint Josemaria would tell you that's just the way to confess you sins, first the biggest one, the one you are most nervous about saying, then the little ones after. And he would remind you how much better you will feel when you are no longer carrying that big rock and all those pebbles.

A Final Note

―――――――――― • ――――――――――

Now you're all set. You know everything you need to know about the Sacrament of Reconciliation. The only thing left now is to DO IT! Do it soon, and do it often.

What a beautiful example we are setting for our family when we ask to go to confession.

Now that we know that confession isn't scary, that's it's easy, comforting, strengthening, and God's will for us, we would be crazy not to go.

An Examination of Conscience

The Commandments are the rules God gave us to help us live in a way that is pleasing to him. The following pages will help us to think about God's love and how it should change our lives and the way we act.

We should use the questions on these pages before we go to confession to help us to remember our sins. It would be even better to read through the questions for one or two commandments each night before we go to bed. That way we will notice if we are committing the same sins over and over again and try harder to avoid those sins.

Each time you do an examination of conscience, start with a short prayer to the Holy Spirit who knows our heart and can help us remember our sins and be sorry for them: *Come Holy Spirit, fill the hearts of your faithful and kindle in them the fire of your love.*

NOTE FOR PARENTS: You know your child well, and can help him prepare for his confession. Feel free to add or remove questions to the ones listed here if you think it is necessary (but take care not to look at what he writes down).

**I am the LORD your God,
you shall have no other gods before me.**

Put God first in your life.

The first commandment reminds us that our love for God should be bigger than anything else in our lives. Jesus said: You shall love the Lord, your God, with all your heart, with all your soul, and with all your mind. This is the greatest and the first commandment. The second is like it: You shall love your neighbor as yourself.[35] Is our love for God the most important thing in our lives?

Ask yourself: Did I remember to say my prayers every day? Did I make time for TV, computer, and friends but not God? Did I put faith in lucky charms, fortunetelling, or other superstitions instead of God? Did I treat churches, priests, and nuns with the proper respect? Did I try to develop my Faith? Do I have confidence in God? Did I ask him for help when I needed to? Do I practice the virtues that come from God: Faith, Hope, and Charity?

....

35   Luke 10:27

**You shall not take the Name
of the LORD your God in vain.**

Be faithful to God in your words.

This commandment reminds us that our words are an important outward sign of our inward love for God.

Ask yourself: Did I do my best to keep any promises I made to God or to others invoking the name of God? Did I remember always to say God's name with love and reverence, never in anger? Did I say things like "Oh my God" or "I swear to God" or "Jesus Christ" as just words, rather than as prayers? Did I say my prayers properly (not too fast and with all my heart)?

Keep holy the Sabbath day.

Rest from work and go to Mass every Sunday and holy day of obligation.

When God created the world, he worked for six days and rested on the seventh. He asks us to do the same thing.

Ask yourself: Did I miss Mass on a Sunday or a holy day of obligation through my own fault? Did I dress nicely for Mass and help my family get there on time? Do I pay attention in church? Do I distract others? Do I try to finish chores and schoolwork in a timely way so that Sunday can be a day of rest and recreation? Do I do something each Sunday to think about God, such as reading the Bible or the lives of the saints, or taking a walk outdoors and admiring God's creation? Do I receive the sacraments of confession and Holy Communion worthily and often?

Honor your father and your mother.

Follow the rules that your parents give you and always treat them with respect.

We learn to obey God by first obeying our parents and other grown-ups with authority over us.

Ask yourself: Was I disobedient to my parents? Did I get mad when they corrected me? Did I fail to show love and respect to them? Did I willingly do my chores and help out around the house? Did I set a good example for my brothers and sisters? Did I obey other grown-ups such as teachers, coaches, and babysitters? Do I complain or have tantrums? Do I pout or drag my feet when my parents ask me to do something? Did I behave outside the home in a way I would not have if my parents were there? Do I help to create an atmosphere of love and joy in my home?

You shall not kill.

Avoid any behavior that can physically harm anyone, including myself.

For this commandment, we need to think about if we have hurt anyone or ourselves, or if we have made other people sin, which could put their souls in danger.

Ask yourself: Did I try to make other people happy? Did I help them when they needed it? Did I fight and hurt anyone physically? Did I tease and hurt anyone's feelings? Did I sit around eating junk food and watching TV instead of eating healthy food and getting exercise? Did I encourage others to do bad things? Did I wish bad things would happen to anyone? Did I refuse to forgive?

You shall not commit adultery.

Show proper respect for the human body and for marriage. Be modest.

This commandment prohibits adultery, which is harming someone's marriage by interfering in the love of the spouses. But it also prohibits any thought or action that goes against purity.

Ask yourself: Did I always dress in a modest and appropriate way? Did I try to get attention for how I look on the outside rather than who I am on the inside? Did I respect my body and other people's bodies? Did I watch TV shows or movies or listen to songs that were disrespectful to women or men? Did I step away if I heard other people having bad conversations or looking at bad things?

You shall not steal.

*Respect the property of others;
get things only in an honest way.*

This one seems pretty self-explanatory, but it goes deeper than we sometimes think.

Ask yourself: Did I take something that did not belong to me from someone else? Remember, stealing covers more than just things you can touch. Did I sneak into a place instead of paying? Did I knowingly sell something for more than it was worth? Did I fail to pay someone when I should have? Did I break or damage something that does not belong to me? Did I return everything that I have borrowed, on time and in good condition? Did I always treat things that belong to other people in my family with respect? Did I cheat on my homework or on a test?

You shall not bear false witness.

*Always tell the truth
about other people.*

Bearing false witness is lying about other people.

Ask yourself: Did I lie about anyone? Did I tell a grown-up that someone else was at fault for something I did? Did I speak up if someone was getting blamed for something he didn't do? Did I suggest that someone might have done something bad when I didn't know for sure? Did I gossip? Did I tell a secret without good reason? Have I been loyal to my friends and family?

Remember: unless necessary or asked to by a grown-up, we should avoid saying bad things about people, even if they are true! Also, if we have hurt someone, his feelings, or his reputation, we should try and make up for it!

You shall not covet your neighbor's wife.

*Be respectful of
other people's relationships
and grateful for your own.*

To covet is to want something that does not belong to you, and especially to wish that you had something instead of the person who has it now. Kids aren't married, but there are still ways we can think about this one.

Ask yourself: Did I get jealous of other people's friends or families? Did I wish that my family was more like someone else's family? Do I thank God for my family and friends and remember to pray for them each day?

You shall not covet your neighbor's goods.

Be content with what you have;
be grateful for the things that God
and other people have given you.

This commandment tells us that we need to be grateful for everything that God has given us and not to worry about what God has given to others.

Ask yourself: Did I thank God and my parents for all the things I have? Did I make my parents feel bad because I wanted things that we can't afford or they think I shouldn't have? Did I want what others have so badly that I made myself sad or angry? Did I treat someone else badly because of my envy? Did I share the things I have with my siblings and with my friends? Did I keep more things than I need rather than giving them away to the poor?

The Sacrament of Penance, a Review

1. The priest will greet you.

2. Make the Sign of the Cross and say, **Bless me Father, for I have sinned**.

3. The priest will invite you to trust in God. He may say, *May the Lord be in your heart and help you to confess your sins with true sorrow.* Then you say, **It has been (the number of weeks or months) since my last confession** and give the priest any other information he should know about you before you tell him your sins.

4. The priest may read or say by heart some words from Scripture about the mercy of God, and repentance.

5. **You tell your sins to the priest.** You may look at your list. The priest might ask you questions to help you.

6. The priest will give you some advice on how to be better, then give you your penance.

7. When the priest asks you to, **say the Act of Contrition** (it's best to have it memorized, but you can read it if necessary).

8. The priest will then give you the absolution saying:

God, the Father of mercies, through the death and resurrection of his Son has reconciled the world to himself and sent the Holy Spirit among us for the forgiveness of sins; through the ministry of the Church may God give you pardon and peace, and I absolve you from your sins in the name of the Father, and of the Son, + and of the Holy Spirit.

You receive absolution by crossing yourself and saying **Amen**.

9. After the absolution, the priest continues: *Give thanks to the Lord, for he is good.*

You answer: **His mercy endures for ever**.

Then the Priest dismisses you by saying:

The Lord has freed you from your sins. Go in peace.

Or he might say:

May the Passion of our Lord Jesus Christ, the intercession of the Blessed Virgin Mary and of all the saints, whatever good you do and suffering you endure, heal your sins, help you to grow in holiness, and reward you with eternal life. Go in peace.

10. Leave the confessional and do your penance immediately.

Under the direction of Romain Lizé, Vice President, MAGNIFICAT

Editor, MAGNIFICAT: Isabelle Galmiche
Editor, Ignatius: Vivian Dudro
Assistant of the Editor: Pascale van de Walle
Layout Designer: Élise Borel
Production: Thierry Dubus, Sabine Marioni

Printed in July 2021 by Graphycems, Spain
Job Number MGN21036-05
Printed in compliance with the Consumer Protection Safety Act of 2008.